San José Public Library  San José Public Library Foundation

———— Thank you ————

SILICON VALLEY
community foundation®

for promoting literacy among
San José children.

NATIVE
AMERICANS

Choctaw

Big Buddy Books

An Imprint of Abdo Publishing
abdopublishing.com

Katie Lajiness

abdopublishing.com

Published by Abdo Publishing, a division of ABDO, PO Box 398166, Minneapolis, Minnesota 55439.
Copyright © 2017 by Abdo Consulting Group, Inc. International copyrights reserved in all countries. No part
of this book may be reproduced in any form without written permission from the publisher. Big Buddy Books™
is a trademark and logo of Abdo Publishing.

Printed in the United States of America, North Mankato, Minnesota.
062016
092016

THIS BOOK CONTAINS
RECYCLED MATERIALS

Cover Photo: © Buddy Mays/Corbis; Shutterstock.com.
Interior Photos: © Danita Delimont/Alamy (p. 5); *Getty Images*: Fort Worth Star-Telegram (p. 27);
    © iStockphoto.com (pp. 11, 25); © Buddy Mays/Corbis (p. 29); © NativeStock.com/AngelWynn
    (pp. 9, 13, 15, 17, 19, 23, 26, 30); Shutterstock.com (p. 21); © Edwin L. Wisherd/National Geographic Creative/
    Corbis (p. 16).

Coordinating Series Editor: Tamara L. Britton
Graphic Design: Adam Craven

Library of Congress Cataloging-in-Publication Data

Lajiness, Katie, author.
    Choctaw / Katie Lajiness.
Minneapolis, MN : ABDO Publishing Company, 2017. | Series:
    Native Americans
LCCN 2015050497| ISBN 9781680781984 | ISBN 9781680774931 (ebook)
LCSH: Choctaw Indians--History--Juvenile literature. | Choctaw
    Indians--Social life and customs--Juvenile literature.
LCC E99.C8 L24 2017 | DDC 976.004/97387--dc23
LC record available at http://lccn.loc.gov/2015050497

CONTENTS

Amazing People

Hundreds of years ago, North America was mostly wild, open land. Native American tribes lived on the land. They had their own languages and **customs**.

The Choctaw (CHAHK-taw) are one Native American tribe. They are known for their hunting and farming skills. Let's learn more about these Native Americans.

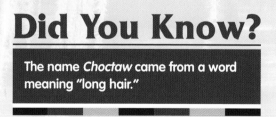

Did You Know?

The name *Choctaw* came from a word meaning "long hair."

Today, the Choctaw still wear traditional clothing and practice their native songs and dances.

5

Choctaw Territory

Choctaw homelands were mostly in what is now Mississippi. Some groups lived near the Mississippi River valley. Tribes also lived in present-day Alabama, Louisiana, and Florida.

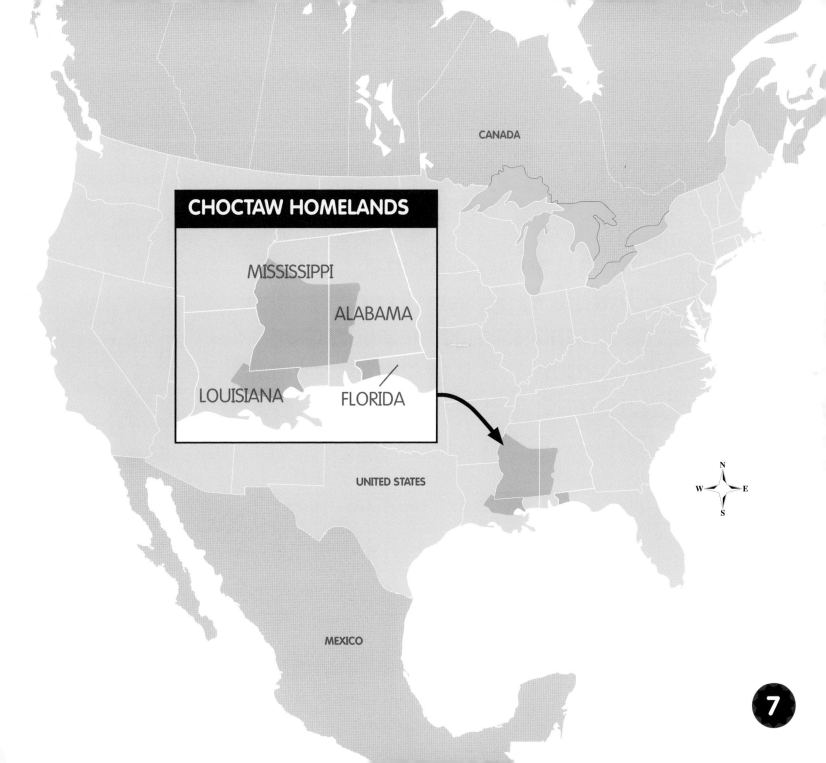

CHOCTAW HOMELANDS

MISSISSIPPI

ALABAMA

LOUISIANA   FLORIDA

CANADA

UNITED STATES

MEXICO

7

HOME LIFE

A Choctaw house was called a *chukka* (CHUH-kuh). One family lived in each chukka. To keep cool, families built their summer homes with grasses. Their warmer winter homes were made of clay.

In the mid-1700s, there were about 70 Choctaw villages. Each had many houses surrounded by farms. And, there was an open area for **ceremonies** and games.

Members of the village worked together to help a family build its winter home.

What They Ate

The Choctaw people were skilled farmers. Corn, beans, pumpkins, and sweet potatoes were common crops. They also gathered wild fruits, nuts, and seeds. Women ground sunflower seeds to make flour.

Choctaw men were talented fishermen and hunters. They caught fish in nearby rivers. And, the men hunted bear, buffalo, and deer.

Did You Know?

The Choctaw called corn, beans, and squash "the three sisters" because they grew well together.

Large deer herds fed the Choctaw throughout the year. One buck could provide more than 50 pounds (23 kg) of meat for the tribe.

11

Daily Life

Choctaw chiefs were fair and wise. They thought of ways to protect their land and people. Chiefs also oversaw the village and planned festivals and dances.

The Choctaw had different clothes depending on the weather. Men wore few clothes in the summer. During the winter, they dressed in leggings, shirts woven from feathers, and moccasins. Women often wore clothes made from deerskin.

 Choctaw women wore deerskin skirts, tops, and moccasins. They completed daily tasks such as preparing food.

Everyone in a Choctaw village had a job to do. Adults often sold or traded extra food for supplies.

Men hunted and brought meat back to the village, often on horseback. Women owned much of the land. And, they did most of the farming.

At a young age, children learned from their parents. And, they helped with daily tasks.

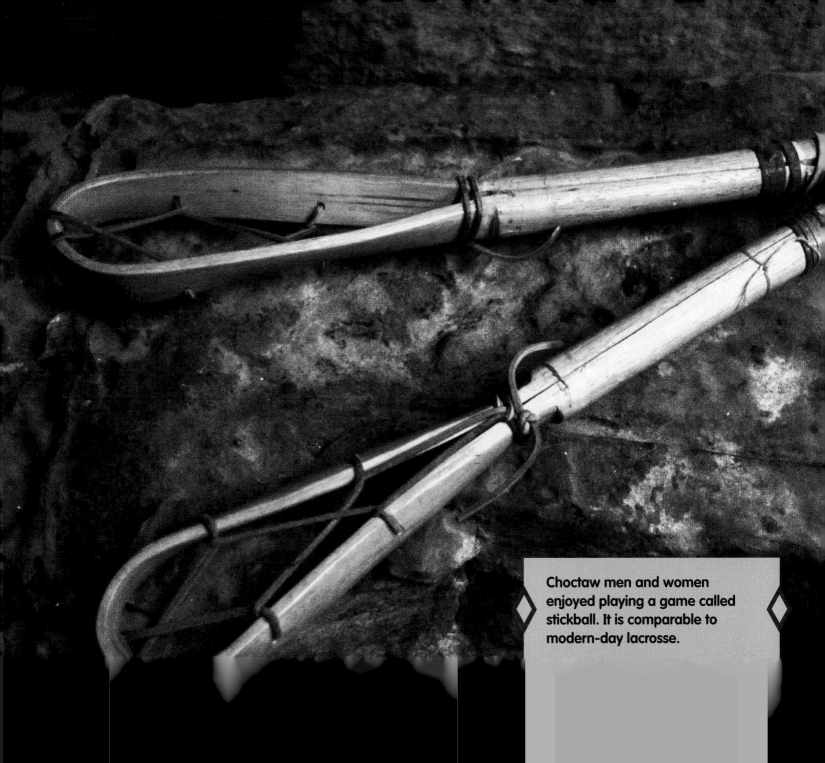

Choctaw men and women enjoyed playing a game called stickball. It is comparable to modern-day lacrosse.

MADE BY HAND

The Choctaw made many objects by hand. They often used natural materials. These arts and crafts added beauty to everyday life.

Baskets

Women wove baskets from river cane that was cut into strips. They used berries, flowers, or roots to dye the cane.

Moccasins

Moccasins were made from deerskin. These shoes were often decorated with beads.

Hunting Tools

 Men used river cane to make blowguns and darts. They used these tools to hunt small animals.

Spirit Life

The Choctaw people held special **ceremonies** and **customs**. They thought sweat would heal their bodies and cleanse their spirits. By pouring water over hot stones, they produced steam to heat their sweathouses.

The tribe honored the sun. They believed the sun had great powers. Out of respect, Choctaw leaders held meetings only on sunny days.

The Choctaw's Green Corn Ceremony lasted four to eight days during the late summer. Every year, they honored the first farm crops by dancing, eating, and praying.

STORYTELLERS

Stories are important to the Choctaw. The tribe's tales were passed down for thousands of years. The people told stories to share their **culture** and history.

In the Choctaw creation story, two brothers called Chata and Chicksah lead their people to a new homeland. When this area becomes too small, the people separate into two tribes. One group goes north and becomes the Chickasaw people. The other group stays and becomes known as the Choctaw.

A famous Choctaw story tells how they began farming corn. The Great Spirit gives corn to the tribe after hungry men share food with her.

21

FIGHTING FOR LAND

For thousands of years, the Choctaw were peaceful people. This changed in 1540. That year, Spanish explorer Hernando de Soto entered Choctaw territory. He tried to take them for **slaves**. The tribe fought the Spanish, and many people died.

After 1700, French explorers arrived. The Choctaw and the French were friendly. And, they often traded goods. The Choctaw fought with the French in the **French and Indian War**. After France lost the war, the British took some of the Choctaw's land.

Hernando de Soto had ten ships and a crew of 700 men. The Choctaw could not win against such a large group.

Chief Pushmataha was a strong Choctaw leader. In 1824, he went to Washington, DC. There, he asked the US government to stop taking more Choctaw land.

In 1830, Congress passed the Indian Removal Act. That same year, the US government and the Choctaw signed a **treaty**. From 1831 to 1833, more than 14,000 Choctaw traveled to Indian Territory. Many people died during their journey. This was known as the Trail of Tears.

During the **American Civil War**, the Choctaw fought with the South. After the war, the US government took more of the tribe's land.

More than 1,000 Choctaw fought for the South during the American Civil War. Some wore soldiers' uniforms. Others wore traditional Choctaw animal skins.

BACK IN TIME

1747–1750

The Choctaw **civil war** was fought. A tribal group wanted to trade with the British instead of the French.

1600s

The Choctaw Nation had more than 20,000 members. It was one of the largest tribes in the Southeast.

1820

The US government wanted more land from the Choctaw. The tribe gave up 5 million acres (2 million ha) from their homeland in Mississippi to the US government.

THE GREAT SEAL

1906

The US government passed the Enabling Act. This declared that Choctaw was no longer a tribe.

1914–1918

During **World War I**, six Choctaw men passed along secret messages by speaking their native language. Few people spoke their language, so enemy countries were unable to break the code.

1960s

The Choctaw tribe regained power to govern itself. More people found jobs. Native **culture** began to thrive, and people practiced their **traditions** again.

The Choctaw Today

The Choctaw have a long, rich history. They are remembered for their farming and hunting skills. Choctaw roots run deep. Today, the people have kept alive those special things that make them Choctaw. Even though times have changed, many people carry the **traditions**, stories, and memories of the past into the present.

Did You Know?

Today, more than 195,000 people are part of the Choctaw tribe.

The Choctaw use feather fans for prayer. These fans are believed to have healing powers.

"I can boast, and say, and tell the truth that none of my fathers or grandfathers, nor any Choctaw ever drew bows against the United States."

– Chief Pushmataha

GLOSSARY

American Civil War the war between the Northern and Southern states from 1861 to 1865.

ceremony a formal event on a special occasion.

civil war a war between groups in the same tribe.

culture (KUHL-chuhr) the arts, beliefs, and ways of life of a group of people.

custom a practice that has been around a long time and is common to a group or a place.

French and Indian War the war between France and Great Britain from 1754 to 1763.

slave a person who is bought and sold as property.

tradition (truh-DIH-shuhn) a belief, a custom, or a story handed down from older people to younger people.

treaty an agreement made between two or more groups.

World War I a war fought in Europe from 1914 to 1918.

WEBSITES

To learn more about Native Americans, visit **booklinks.abdopublishing.com**. These links are routinely monitored and updated to provide the most current information available.

INDEX